My Money

Ellen K. Mitten

ROURKE PUBLISHING
www.rourkepublishing.com

www.rourkepublishing.com

PHOTO CREDITS: Cover: © Mike Kemp; Title Page, 5: © AVAVA; Page 3: © Bryan Busovicki; Page 7: © Kenishirotie; Page 9: © Michael Coddington; Page 10: © Associated Press, Jack Dempsey; Page 11: © Vova Pomortzeff; Page 12: © STILLFX; Page 14, 15: © Renee Brady; Page 17: © Georgios Kollidas, © RagnaRock; Page 17: © Robynrg; Page 19: © CandyBoxPhotos; Page 21: © MarcusPhoto1; Page 22: © Bryan Busovicki, © Kenishirotie; Page 23: © Georgios Kollidas, © Associated Press, Jack Dempsey, © AVAVA

Edited by Meg Greve

Cover design by Renee Brady
Interior design by Renee Brady

Library of Congress Cataloging-in-Publication Data

Mitten, Ellen.
  My money / Ellen K. Mitten.
    p. cm. -- (Little world social studies)
  Includes bibliographical references and index.
  ISBN 978-1-61590-330-6 (Hard Cover) (alk. paper)
  ISBN 978-1-61590-569-0 (Soft Cover)
  1. Money--United States--Juvenile literature. I. Title.
  HG501.M58 2011
  332.4'973--dc22
                                    2010009265

Rourke Publishing
Printed in the United States of America, North Mankato, Minnesota
033010
033010LP

www.rourkepublishing.com - rourke@rourkepublishing.com
Post Office Box 643328 Vero Beach, Florida 32964

Long ago, people had to **barter**, or trade, one thing for another thing to get the **goods** they needed.

Now, people use money to buy goods.

My money is made up of **coins** and **bills**.

My coins are made, or **minted**, from different metals.

At the U.S. Mint, metals are poured into coin molds, punched out by size, and then stamped on both sides.

Coin	Heads and Tails	How Much Is It Worth?
Penny		1¢
Nickel		5¢
Dime		10¢
Quarter		25¢
Half-Dollar		50¢

U.S. Mint. Denver, Colorado

The U.S. Mint molds and stamps over 20 million coins each day.

Which U.S. Mint is closest to your house?

U.S. Mints That Make Coins

☆ Denver, Colorado

☆ San Francisco, California

★ Philadelphia, Pennsylvania

The government prints my paper money. Paper money comes in different **dollar** values.

Value	What Does It Look Like?	Who Is Pictured On It?
$1.00		George Washington
$2.00		Thomas Jefferson

$5.00		Abraham Lincoln
$10.00		Alexander Hamilton
$20.00		Andrew Jackson
$50.00		Ulysses S. Grant
$100.00		Benjamin Franklin

The dollar is the basic unit of my money. A one dollar bill is the same as 100 cents.

100¢

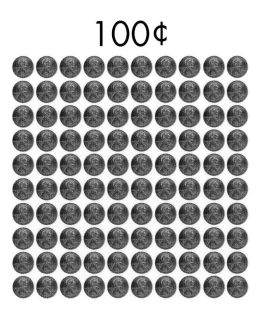

=

$1.00

My money is used to buy all types of goods and **services**.

My money is changing. Instead of using coins and bills to buy things, sometimes we use credit cards or debit cards.

Picture Glossary

 **barter** (BAR-tur): To trade by exchanging food or other goods or services. People used to barter before there was money.

 **bills** (BILS): A piece of paper money. The one dollar bill is worth 100 cents.

 **coins** (KOINS): Small pieces of metal stamped with a design and used as money.

dollar (DOL-ur): The main unit of money in the United States, Canada, Australia, and New Zealand.

goods (GUDZ): Things that are sold, or things that someone owns.

minted (MINT-id): To make coins out of metal. Coins in the U.S. are made at the U.S. Mint.

Index

Websites

www.usmint.gov/kids

www.federalreserve.gov/kids

www.kids.gov

About the Author

Ellen K. Mitten has been teaching four and five year-olds since 1995. She and her family love reading all sorts of books!